BMX Bikes

By Kathleen W. Deady

Consultant:
Moniqua Plante
ESPN X Games

CAPSTONE
HIGH-INTEREST
BOOKS

an imprint of Capstone Press
Mankato, Minnesota

Capstone High-Interest Books are published by Capstone Press
151 Good Counsel Drive, P.O. Box 669, Mankato, Minnesota 56002
http://www.capstone-press.com

Library of Congress Cataloging-in-Publication Data
Deady, Kathleen W.
   BMX bikes/Kathleen W. Deady.
   p. cm.—(Wild rides!)
   Includes bibliographical references and index.
   ISBN 0-7368-0925-2
   1. BMX bikes—Juvenile literature. [1. BMX bikes. 2. Bicycle motocross.]
I. Title. II. Series.
TL437.5.B58 D43 2002
629.227'2—dc21   2001000208

Summary: Discusses these small bikes, their history, parts, and competitions.

Editorial Credits
Matt Doeden, editor; Karen Risch, product planning editor; Kia Bielke,
   cover and interior designer; Katy Kudela, photo researcher

Photo Credits
ALLSPORT PHOTOGRAPHY, 10–11, 14 (top), 20 (top), 24, 26
David F. Clobes, 16
Isaac Hernandez/Mercury Press, cover
Patrick Batchelder, 7, 20 (bottom)
Shazamm, 22
SportsChrome-USA/Rob Tringali Jr., 4 (top), 4 (bottom), 8, 12, 28; Michael
Zito, 14 (bottom), 18

1 2 3 4 5 6 07 06 05 04 03 02

Table of Contents

Learn about:

- **BMX bike shapes**

- **Cost of BMX bikes**

- **Races and competitions**

CHAPTER 1

BMX Bikes

Eight BMX riders line up to begin a race. The racers pedal hard and fast as the starting gate drops. They hold their bodies low on their bikes as they ride over a series of bumps. Dirt flies up behind their tires as they skid through sharp turns.

The riders approach a large dirt jump. They pull up slightly on their handlebars as they reach the top of the jump. The riders then sail through the air. Some riders do stunts while in the air. They take their hands off the handlebars. Others take their feet off the pedals. The riders land on the other side of the jump and speed to the finish line.

About BMX Bikes

BMX stands for bicycle motocross. Riders use BMX bikes in races and to perform stunts. BMX bikes are smaller than most bikes. They have wide tires that are designed to ride over rough ground.

BMX racing bikes are shaped like motorcycles. The bikes have small, low frames. The frames are lightweight and strong. They have high handlebars that slant backward.

Many companies make BMX bikes. Schwinn, GT, Haro, and Yamaha are among the most popular BMX manufacturers. Most BMX bikes cost about $150. But a top racing or stunt BMX bike may cost more than $3,000.

BMX Bikes in Action

Riders of all ages can enjoy BMX bikes. Most people ride them just for fun. They may race on dirt tracks near their homes. They may try some simple stunts. Groups of BMX riders may gather to compare different stunts.

Some riders join organized races and other competitions. Some cities have special tracks and parks just for BMX riders. BMX groups may host organized races. They award trophies and prizes to the winners.

Skilled riders may become professionals. Professional riders take part in BMX competitions around the world. Some riders compete in BMX races. Others take part in stunt riding competitions. Professional riders earn their living by taking part in these competitions.

BMX bikes are small and sturdy.

Learn about:

- Motocross racing

- Early BMX races

- Changes in the sport

CHAPTER 2

Early Models of BMX Bikes

BMX racing grew out of the sport of motocross racing. Motocross racers ride dirt bikes with small motors on dirt tracks. Bicycle riders began racing on the same tracks. They called this new sport "bicycle motocross." Racers shortened that name to BMX.

A New Sport

Early BMX racers tried racing with regular bicycles. But these bicycles could not handle the rough motocross tracks. Wheels, spokes, and fenders bent too easily. Bike frames broke and pedals cracked. Riders often had trouble controlling the bicycles.

People began changing their bicycles for BMX racing. They built bikes with small frames. They added small, wide tires. They removed the fenders and chain guards.

In 1970, a motorcycle movie called *On Any Sunday* became popular. The movie's popularity increased interest in motocross and BMX racing. Soon, bicycle manufacturers such as

Schwinn began building bikes especially for BMX racing.

Early BMX bikes were different from other types of bicycles. Riders had to learn how to handle the small, sturdy bikes. Riders quickly learned that BMX bikes could take much rougher treatment than normal bicycles.

BMX bikes can take much rougher treatment than normal bicycles.

BMX Changes

All early BMX competitions were races. At first, riders tried to stay on the ground over the bumps. But soon, they began to use larger mounds of dirt. They tried to jump high in the air before landing.

Freestyle bicycle stunt riding is a popular sport today.

Some riders performed stunts while they were in the air. The stunts did not help the riders win races. But the fans enjoyed watching the stunts. People cheered as the riders turned and twisted in the air.

Riders also began to practice stunts on the ground. Many BMX riders learned stunts by watching skateboarders. They started to try similar moves with their bikes. This sport became known as freestyle BMX. Today, most people call the sport freestyle bicycle stunt riding.

Freestyle riding was even harder on bikes than racing was. Some of the racing BMX bikes could not handle the rough treatment. In 1983, Haro built the first BMX bikes made especially for freestyle riding. The bikes had stronger, heavier frames. The frames allowed riders to do more difficult stunts. These new stunts helped increase the popularity of freestyle bicycle stunt riding.

In 1995, freestyle bicycle stunt riding was part of the first X Games. The ESPN TV network organizes this extreme sports competition every year.

Learn about:

- **BMX power**

- **Racing and freestyle bike differences**

- **BMX tires**

CHAPTER 3

Designing a BMX Bike

Today, bicycle manufacturers build two main types of BMX bikes. They build racing bikes for speed. They build stunt riding bikes to be strong and sturdy.

Frame

The main body of a BMX bike is the frame. The seat, wheels, and handlebars connect to the frame. Many racing bikes are made of a lightweight metal called aluminum. Most stunt riding bikes are made of a metal called chromoly steel alloy. This metal is a mix of the metals chromium and molybdenum.

Three metal tubes form a BMX bike's main triangle.

All BMX frames have the same basic shape. Three metal tubes join to form a triangle. The tubes are called a top tube, a down tube, and a seat tube. Two more tubes form the front fork. These tubes connect to the front wheel.

A rear triangle connects to the back of the main triangle. It includes two tubes called seat stays and two tubes called chain stays. The seat stays connect to the seat. The chain stays connect to the rear wheel.

Drivetrain

A simple drivetrain powers BMX bikes. The bikes have only one gear. Riders power the bikes with pedals joined to metal arms called cranks. The cranks connect to the bike's front sprocket. This turning device includes metal teeth that connect to the bike's chain.

The rider pedals to turn the front sprocket. The sprocket then turns the chain. The chain is connected to a smaller rear sprocket. This sprocket connects to the wheel. It turns the wheel to power the bike.

Most freestyle riders add pegs to their wheel axles.

Wheels and Brakes

BMX bikes have small wheels. Strong metal rings fit inside the tires and support them.

BMX racing bikes use knobby tires. These tires have deep tread. This pattern of bumps and grooves grips dirt tracks. Freestyle riders do not need tires with deep tread. Instead, they use extra wide tires. The extra width increases the bike's balance. Extra balance helps riders land after stunts such as flips and spins.

Most freestyle riders add pegs to their wheel axles. Pegs help riders balance on their bikes during stunts. Riders also use pegs to slide across obstacles such as railings and curbs.

Brakes connect to the wheels. Racing bikes usually have only rear caliper brakes. These brakes slow the bike by squeezing the rear tire rim. Freestyle bikes have both front and rear caliper brakes. Freestyle riders use the front brakes to perform some balancing stunts.

Learn about:

- ■ **BMX tracks**

- ■ **Forms of stunt riding**

- ■ **Safety**

CHAPTER 4

BMX Bikes in Competition

In 1974, riders formed the National Bicycle League (NBL). The American Bicycle Association (ABA) began in 1977. These two groups organize BMX competitions. They also create rules and standards for riders to follow. They try to keep the sport popular and safe.

BMX Racing

BMX races are called motos. They take place on hard-packed dirt tracks. The tracks are usually about 800 to 1,400 feet (240 to 430 meters) long. Racers begin at a starting gate at the top of a hill. The racers ride around the track once.

Racing tracks have a mix of bumps, jumps, and berms. A bump is a small mound of dirt. Larger mounds of dirt are called jumps. Riders may speed over jumps and sail through the air. A sloped pile of dirt on a corner is called a berm. The berm's slope helps racers turn sharp corners without slowing down.

Street riders compete on park courses.

Racers must win more than one race to win an event. Many racers may take part in each competition. The tracks are not large enough for all the riders to compete at once. Riders begin with qualifying races. These races are called heats. The top finishers in each heat advance to the next race. The winner of the final heat is the event champion.

Street Riding

BMX stunt riders may take part in several types of competitions. Street riding is the oldest type of freestyle competition. Early street riders performed stunts on city streets and in parks. They performed stunts on railings, stairs, and curbs.

Today, street riders compete on special courses called park courses. These courses include obstacles such as ramps and stair railings. Judges give riders scores based on the stunts they perform. Riders must do a variety of stunts in a set amount of time. They must use many obstacles.

Vert Riding

Vert riding is another type of stunt riding competition. Vert riders perform stunts on half-pipe ramps during these competitions. A half-pipe ramp is shaped like the letter

Riders use the half-pipe's curved walls to jump high in the air.

"U." Riders use the half-pipe's curved walls to jump high in the air. They perform stunts while in the air. These stunts are called aerials. Riders also use the top edge of the ramp to perform stunts. This metal edge is called coping.

Vert riders have a set amount of time to perform their stunts. Judges give them scores based on the style and difficulty of the stunts they complete.

Other Forms of Stunt Riding

Street riding and vert riding are the most popular forms of stunt riding. But many riders also take part in flatland riding and dirt jumping.

Flatland riders perform stunts on flat, paved surfaces. They do not use obstacles. In competition, riders must do a series of tricks. They perform these tricks by balancing their feet on the pedals, frame, pegs, and tires. Riders do not touch the ground while performing these tricks.

In dirt jumping, riders perform aerial stunts off dirt jumps. Riders each get at least three turns to perform stunts. Riders receive points based on the style and difficulty of their stunts.

**Riders protect themselves with helmets,
gloves, and pads.**

Safety

Safety is important to BMX riders. Groups such as the ABA set safety rules for competitions. Officials inspect tracks and bikes before each event. Racers make sure their bikes are in perfect working order. They make sure all of the parts are tightly fitted and in good shape.

Most riders add padding to their bikes. One pad covers the handlebars. Another pad covers the bar that supports the handlebars. A third pad covers the top tube of the bike frame. These pads protect riders during accidents.

Riders also wear safety clothing. They wear helmets to protect against head injuries. Riders wear long pants to protect their legs during crashes. Gloves protect riders' hands. Most riders also wear knee pads, elbow pads, and shin guards. This safety gear helps BMX riders enjoy their sport safely.

Dave Mirra

Dave Mirra is one of the world's most popular BMX stunt riders. Many people believe Mirra is the best stunt rider in the world. His nickname is "Miracle Boy."

Mirra was born April 4, 1974, in Syracuse, New York. He began racing BMX bikes in 1984. He began competing in freestyle events in 1987. He quickly became one of the best stunt riders in the world.

Mirra is one of the most successful athletes in the history of the X Games. From 1996 to 2000, he won 12 X Games medals. No other athlete had won that many medals.

Mirra made history in the park competition at the 2000 X Games in San Francisco. He landed the first double back flip in competition. Many riders had believed this stunt was impossible.

Words to Know

aerial (AIR-ee-uhl)—a stunt performed in the air

aluminum (uh-LOO-mi-nuhm)—a lightweight, silver-colored metal; many racing BMX bike frames are made of aluminum.

berm (BURM)—a banked turn or corner on a BMX track

calipers (KAL-uh-purss)—a set of clamps at the end of a brake cable; calipers press against a wheel to stop it from turning.

chromoly (KROH-muh-lee)—a mixture of two metals called chromium and molybdenum; some BMX bike frames are made of chromoly.

drivetrain (DRIVE-trane)—the part of a vehicle that provides power to the axles

frame (FRAYM)—the body of a bike

sprocket (SPROK-it)—a wheel with a rim made of toothlike points that fit into the holes of a bicycle chain

tread (TRED)—a series of bumps and deep grooves on a tire; tread helps tires grip surfaces.

To Learn More

Glaser, Jason. *Bicycle Stunt Riding.* Extreme Sports. Mankato, Minn.: Capstone High-Interest Books, 1999.

Hayhurst, Chris. *Bicycle Stunt Riding! Catch Air.* The Extreme Sports Collection. New York: Rosen Central, 2000.

Useful Addresses

American Bicycle Association
P.O. Box 718
Chandler, AZ 85244

Canadian BMX Association
3175 Sion Frontage Road
Grand Forks, BC V0H 1H0
Canada

National Bicycling League
3958 Brown Park Drive
Suite D
Hilliard, OH 43026

Internet Sites

American Bicycle Association
http://www.ababmx.com

Canadian BMX Association
http://www.canadianbmx.com

EXPN.com
http://expn.go.com

Index